FIGHT FIRED WITH HIM FIRE

BY MEGAN WAGNER

Copyright © 2017 by Megan Wagner

All rights reserved. No part of this book may be reproduced in any form or by any electronic or mechanical means, including information storage retrieval systems, without permission in writing from the author, except by a reviewer who may quote brief passages in a review.

ISBN-13: 978-1973888444
ISBN-10: 1973888440

This book is dedicated to those who are on the down and outs; who are terrifyingly standing at the beginning of a new chapter; and who dare to rise from the ashes to create a career (and life) that is irreversibly true to your calling.

Hang in there. It will get better.

Table of Contents

Free Download: Job Loss Resource Guide 7

Prologue 9

Chapter 1 Your Career Has Just Imploded 15

Chapter 2 The Smoldering Aftermath 33

Chapter 3 Extinguishing the Flames 49

Chapter 4 Igniting Your Passions 71

A Final Note 91

Acknowledgments 95

About the Author 97

How I Did It 100

Free Download: Job Loss Resource Guide

As a special bonus, we're offering readers a FREE job loss resource guide filled with helpful tools, websites, publications and more. We personally used these and hope they will help you navigate through your job loss journey!

meganmwagner.com/job-loss-guide

Prologue

Job loss sucks for anyone. No matter your life situation, whether you're married or single, have kids or no kids, own a home or rent an apartment, it can be the scariest time in your life and certainly can be viewed as a significant career setback. According to the US Bureau of Labor Statistics, in January 2017 alone, over 51,000 employees lost their jobs due to layoff or firings *each day*. That's over 1.6 million people who are worried about finances, reputation and what is going to happen next. Little do they know, this temporary moment in time could be the best thing that has ever happened to them.

If you've recently experienced job loss, you may not know where to turn for words of encouragement, what to do next, or how to overcome this obstacle. *Fighting FIRED with Fire* will show you that you're not alone in this career transition. This book offers readers relatable stories from those who have experienced job loss, tips for dealing with the emotional impact of job loss and how you can turn this temporary setback into a silver lining for your career and your life. Readers who have experienced job loss may be in an emotional fog, have no idea where to start or what to do to get back on track, which is why we've included four easy-to-follow action plans to guide you on a successful transition.

As an eleven-year marketing communications

professional, I've always dreamed of a more meaningful career and owning my own business. Then one fateful day, that dream was forced into fruition, when I was let go from my job as a communications director. I felt a million different emotions over the next few months—everything from relief to anxiety and fear. I didn't have a clue what to do next except get to work and build the business I had always wanted to create. Nearly two years later, I've come to realize that my dismissal was the best thing that could have happened to me and am living my dream of owning my own marketing consulting business.

Readers who have recently experienced job loss will learn from my own trip-ups and successes in my job-loss journey, along with many stories of others who have been down this same transition. You'll read about the variety of emotions to expect over the next few months and how to constructively cope with them. I'll also provide some insights on getting back on your career track, exploring new opportunities and igniting passions to turn them in to a career you love.

Job loss is one of the most stressful experiences that someone can go through. I promise that after reading this book, you will find comfort in knowing that you're not alone, that you can overcome this temporary career setback and go on to experience a meaningful career that you've always dreamed of. Using four easy-to-follow action plans, I'll help guide you step-by-step through the stages of job loss and offer simple yet helpful advice on getting through this trying time successfully.

If you're one of the 51,000 daily employees who have

either been laid off or fired, don't wait in fear and panic about the future. Don't be the person to wallow in self-pity. Show your friends, loved ones and colleagues that you're a survivor they can be proud of. Prove to yourself that you are fearless and can overcome anything. Time is precious and we only have one shot at this life. The sun will still rise in the East tomorrow so get up, dust yourself off and start the next exciting chapter of your career today!

The career re-building and passion igniting tips, tricks and stories will encourage and inspire you to take action and let success be your ultimate revenge. All you have to do is read each section, follow the action plans at the end of each chapter and hold yourself accountable. That's it! Take control of your career, know you're not alone and blaze a new career path that you've always dreamed of.

Chapter 1
Your Career Has Just Imploded

"All we can do is keep breathing ..."
—Ingrid Michelson

June 25, 2015 is a day I'll always remember and wish I could forever forget. I had been employed as a communications director for nearly four and a half years. The day didn't feel right from the get go when I began my thirty-minute commute. And just like that, I was summoned to a brief meeting with my supervisor and HR representative and was notified that my employment was ending.

I've read that your gut is right about 90 percent of the time, so I had suspected something was going on. Several other company employees had been let go that year for a variety of reasons. Employee morale was at an all-time low. Now it was my turn to walk the plank (sans rum in hand—that came later).

Now I know what parolees feel like before being released from jail. Scared. Relived. Nervous. Hopeful. If you've been there, then you know what I'm talking about. I quietly and calmly packed up my office after the meeting, not shedding a single tear or shouting a single curse word. Over my dead body would they see me get emotional. I wouldn't give them the satisfaction. Stubbornness had always been one of my strong suits and I wasn't about to back down now.

The rest of the afternoon was a blur. I called my closest work friends, both past and present, to share the news of my undoing. They were stunned and angry as I was. The conversations I had with six amazing friends were just what I needed to get through one of the most difficult days in recent times. Their overwhelming support and encouragement were exactly what I needed in the first few hours that my life, career and future were in a tailspin.

I don't remember being overly emotional that day. My relief from leaving a toxic workplace was certainly greater than my fear. Like a huge weight was being lifted off of my shoulders. Over the past year or so (hell, maybe longer) I had been plunging into a rampant cycle of unhappiness. My health was declining. The number on the scale was going up. I was overly angry and moody all the time. I could always predict when I was going to get sick with a bad head cold. I rarely laughed. Complaining was an hourly occurrence. I had become the worst version of myself I never wanted to be. I wasn't *me* and it was pure misery.

I can't count the number of times I daydreamed of quitting my job, selling my house, packing up my dog, moving to the Caribbean and spending the rest of my life serving fancy tropical drinks with umbrellas. Everyone has that dream, right? I'd be the female version of Tom Cruise in *Cocktail*, slinging drinks and flirting with tourists. I would hop on different job searching websites and look for jobs in the US Virgin Islands. It was when I actually started applying for jobs in Saint Thomas and my daydream started seeping into reality, I knew something had to change. And the universe changed it for me.

So that afternoon, I pretended to live my daydream. It was a sunny, warm afternoon so I turned on some Reggae music, put on my straw fedora, picked up a bottle of Captain Morgan's finest and chillaxed on the back patio—at three in the afternoon. My neighbors probably thought I had lost my mind. Even my dog was giving me a funny look. I had turned into a "Desperate Housewife of Erie County" in a matter of an hour.

When my husband came home later that day, I told him, with a huge smile on my face, that I'd been forced into early retirement.

"Pack your bags, dammit, we're moving to Turks and Caicos!" I slurred, with the spiced perfume of Captain Morgan on my breath.

He put his work bag down and sat down on our outdoor couch with a look of sheer panic on his face, a look I'll never forget, knowing good and well he couldn't support both of us on his salary.

"We'll be fine. We'll be fine, I promise," I said, doing my very best to reassure him, even when I wasn't too reassured myself. We had always needed both of our incomes to cover household expenses and now with a big chunk of that gone, we needed to figure something out fast.

I knew deep down that I had a bigger purpose. And so it began. I embarked on the scariest, freeing, unnerving, exciting time in my life. Ready or not.

Surviving the F-Bomb

Does my story sound familiar? If it does, first of all, I'm sorry this happened to you. I totally get that you're most likely feeling a million different things right now. It might be, up to this point in your life, the most stressful event you've ever experienced. You're probably wondering how your family will react, how you'll make your next mortgage payment, or when you'll find work again. Job loss affects a person in many different ways. Of course, our minds automatically go to the financial challenge someone faces. But there are other factors that impact a person's frame of mind. Individuals may be dealing with the emotional struggles that come with the notion of being rejected or perception that you weren't needed anymore, the social challenges when you're out with friends and family and feel shame over losing your job.

It's crazy scary but the good news is that you still have air in your lungs and a beating heart. Yay!

Public relations and social media pro, Jason Mollica, has been on the receiving end of being let go from his job but proves that you can overcome any challenge that job loss brings. I had the chance to chat with him about his experience coping with job loss and how he recovered and rebuilt his career.

"It took me a little bit to actually come to grips with being let go," he explains. "I had always left on my own terms because of a new position or moving. These days, I have a much better outlook. While I said in the initial months and years that I was fine, I wasn't. I harbored resentment. It's much different now. I was able to make my consultancy work and enjoy what I do on a daily basis. The frustration of being let go has turned into a bit of appreciation now."

As you read this book, there is only one thing you need to do. KEEP MOVING FORWARD. Keep moving forward through the book and also through life. One foot in front of the other. Whether it's big steps or baby steps, make sure those steps don't move backwards. Just like Dory from *Finding Nemo*, keep the mantra, "Just keep swimming, just keep swimming …"

Job loss Statistics

Over 51,000 employees each day are frightened about what the future is going to hold. Over 51,000 who are terrified about how they're going to tell their spouses, loved ones and friends. Over 51,000 who have no idea how they'll pay their next car payment or mortgage. Over 51,000 who have children or parents to support. I highlight this "doom and gloom" to make a very important point.

You're not in this alone.

Since the beginning of industrialized America, people have been and always will lose their jobs. You were not the first and you will certainly not be the last. Some of the most famous and recognizable names have been fired. Peyton Manning and Tony Dungy (two of my favorite former Colts!), Steve Jobs, Oprah Winfrey, Mark Cuban, JK Rowling, and Anna Wintour, who famously stated, "I recommend that you all get fired. It's a great learning experience." That's just to name a few.

Human resources expert Jody Sirianni is one of my favorite people. Now the Vice President of Human Resources for an elder care facility, she has seen it all in the workplace, having worked in HR for 22 years and handled over 500 layoffs, eliminations and terminations. Jody has had to close down warehouses, labs, and full departments. She sat down with me and explained how elimination decisions are made and shed light on the job loss perspective from an HR standpoint.

"As I'm going through the process and working with the managers or the executives to make the determination of who is going to be eliminated, it's very matter-of-fact," she said. "You have to make a decision. My job as the HR person is to make sure that the company is legally protected, that we're picking the right person, that all the ducks are in a row, so to speak, to make that decision."

While the process may sound a bit cold and unemotional, the impacts of the decisions certainly aren't lost on the people who are delivering the unfortunate news.

"As you start kind of forming the elimination list, it becomes really hard," she explains. "After all these years, it still bothers me that I have to do job eliminations. But my job as an HR professional is to always have empathy, and do it in the most respectful and fastest way possible so that it's easier on the employee."

Jody also went on to say that the ultimate goal of an HR professional is not to draw it out or make the person feel less than who they are or that they're horrible people. She tries to give them a lot of respect and a lot of empathy. But at the end of the day, she ultimately has to do her job and needs to be very business-like.

We've talked ad nauseam about why companies eliminate positions, how broken the workplace is and how most companies are failing miserably at keeping up with a diverse workforce. Since Jody has a plethora of HR experience, I decided she would be the perfect person to explain why job loss happens and how dismissed employees can recover their career.

"There's a certainly a responsibility for the company to identify any employment issues early on," she states. "I think what happens far too often in organizations is that managers, in particular, put their head in the sand and don't want to deal with the issues. So the issues starts as a little pebble, they just ignore it and ignore it and it becomes bigger and bigger and becomes a boulder. And then all the sudden they're like 'I want this person gone.' Well, if you would have dealt with it six months ago, you wouldn't have had this boulder of a problem and now you want the person to get fired because you weren't managing it."

But at the end of the day, and no matter who is to be faulted, you're out of a job.

This new chapter in your career (and your life) is happening whether you like it or not. How you handle your emotions to rise above, put the pieces back together and create a career you love again is completely up to you. So here's to getting back up off the ground and taking life by the horns!

When I was coming up for the vision of this book, I wanted you to hear from a wide variety of perspectives from those who have been there in your shoes. I sent out a call for people of all different walks of life to share their experiences coping with job loss. In the next section, you'll read the heartbreaking, unjust and liberating stories about the day they found themselves unemployed.

I knew that I didn't want this book to be all about me and my job loss story. Hearing stories and experiences from my friends and colleagues who had been through the same thing helped me get through that crazy scary and uncertain time more than anything and so I wanted to include the narratives of others with the readers of this book. You will find that there are job loss experiences that are far worse or way better than your situation. Here are their own words about the day they found themselves out of a job.

"It was over the phone because we (government contractors) had not been brought back to work during the time the government was shut down in October, 2013. I was told there was not going to be enough money in the budget once the contract was renegotiated to keep my position and that of approximately twenty others. I was in management so understood that it was more cost effective for the company to lose my position as opposed to that of three lesser paid employees. There was no time to prepare and what was worse, my benefits (medical and dental) were suspended immediately. There was no warning. I felt that aspect was completely unfair."

"The day I was let go was a relief! But the events leading

up to that day were horrible and the worst of my life."

"I was a senior trainer for a global company and provided classroom training and supported projects. Employees off the shop floor came to me about being harassed by supervisors and HR. I stood up for them and despite a perfect performance record, I was fired. In my 28 years with the company, I had never been disciplined for anything and my performance appraisals often were at 'role model' level, including the last one I received right before getting fired. Kansas is a Right-to-Work state. You can be fired without reason. HR fired me and simply told me I was no longer needed. After 28 years, I was fired with no severance."

"This was very early in my career. I was called into the Sales Manager's office (I actually reported to the CEO, but he was nowhere to be found). He told me that I was being laid off effective immediately, given two weeks salary. When I asked for a letter of recommendation, he told me he could write a personal one, but not one on company letterhead. I was in my mid-twenties, single, with no family around to help. It scared the daylights out of me. After a few days, I decided to move to a larger city, and started working for a temp agency there. Somehow, working two and three jobs, I made enough to pay for rent and food. Turns out, that's where I met my future husband!"

"Fortunately, my general manager seemed very compassionate, and advised it was only due to financial difficulties in the industry. I now believe it was just lots of words."

"My manager and I were called into a meeting with the COO—we both saw it coming. He claimed they were discussing restructuring and possibly outsourcing our department and our services were no longer needed."

"I was completely blindsided and was the top performer in company. The company gave no answers to any questions I had."

"I was having a great day then got into an argument and then got fired."

"This was the first job I had, really, out of college. I was a secretary and was laid off. I was sad but had other prospects. I don't think I worried too much because I was confident of my skills and had networked. I had a job within a week. The second time I was jobless, I left on mutual terms. The work situation was beyond miserable. I thought I would branch out and try my own thing. That didn't work out so well! I was without a job for several months and was financially insecure. I went into a bit of debt on that one and am not proud of it, but it is what it is. I'm employed and doing well now!"

"I was called on a Monday to ask me to meet with the vice president the next day at 9:00 a.m. I said I had an outside meeting until 9:30 and would be in right after, he was fine with that. I had a premonition that he was up to something. The next day I came into my office and my computer would not work, so that gave me my first clue. I went down to the corporate office and the VP was waiting for me. He said that I was being let go because I didn't fit into their plans for the future. He said they had hired someone who had more experience and would take them to the next level. I said thank you very much and left to go back to my office to pack. I called my team in to my office and told them I was let go. Answered their questions and gave them a positive talk, thanked them all for their hard work and dedication. I then invited my team to go to lunch with me at a restaurant near us after I finished packing. Finished packing and went down to the corporate office, walked in handed over my keys and walked out! Met my team for lunch and never looked back! I'm proud of what I accomplished and achieved, I hold my head up high!

"It was pretty clear that my boss and I were not necessarily seeing eye-to-eye. I wanted to see our small firm look more into social marketing. But, it ended up being a dead end. That was just one instance of the gap that was widening. It was the day after the Labor Day holiday in the US and I helped my daughter onto the bus for her first day of first grade. I got into work a few minutes late, which was previously known. Before I could even sit down, my boss asked if I would come into his office. He shut the door, asked about my daughter, and then began to list reasons things weren't working out. I always believed that anything could be fixed. But, this wasn't going to be fixed. After about two minutes of listening to my boss list why he wasn't happy, I said, 'Can we get to the point of why I'm in here?' He said, 'We're letting you go.' I had never, ever been canned, fired, let go, whatever. I walked out of his office, into mine and, then, gathered my things. I felt empty, angry. As I left and got into my car, I thought, *Well, this changes a few things*. It did. As angry and empty as I felt, I called my wife to tell her the news. She was shocked. But she said the words I'll never forget. 'Well, now you can start your business.' It took a bit for the sting and frustration of getting let go out of my system, but that day started a new chapter of my life."

"I got a severance package after years of hell in a government job. I was on stress leave and they refused to accept the medical evidence so I was without income for several months and my union wasn't helpful. It was actually a relief to get the package even though I had no idea what would come next."

"I arrived 25 minutes late for my shift. My boss waited until he had to leave for the day, which was a couple hours earlier than when I left, to walk me to the door and ask me for my badge. I was the only person in my department earlier in the day, so they didn't want to let me go then. Waited until other workers came back from being on the road to 'let me go.' I would have preferred if it was done right away. I felt more used the way it happened. I had been late before, not my first time. I own that and am not using an excuse. But, I feel like if I hadn't come forward about the sexual harassment from a coworker, I wouldn't have been let go."

"I actually knew it was coming, but it was still pretty upsetting."

"It was by the book. Every (UK) law was followed. I was last to go from my team so I was prepared."

"There was a meeting put on my calendar so I showed up

and the person I was supposed to meet with wasn't there so I was worried about her. I waited a bit and then her superior walked in so I thought something bad happened to her. Come to find out it was a fake meeting notice, set up to get me there to tell me my department was being eliminated. Then HR came in and explained the details."

See? You're not the first and certainly not the last person to go through this trying time. No matter how you look at it, being told you're no longer employed, no matter what the circumstance, flat out sucks. So what do you do now? In the next section, I will give you a clear and concise plan to get you through the initial shock of losing your job.

* * *

When I was writing this book, I looked at it from the perspective of what I would have wanted to read in a book right after I lost my job. Fresh off of my professional banishment, I had no clue what to do, where to begin, what steps to take or how to build a plan for myself going forward. So I thought adding easy-to-follow actions plans at the end of every section would be a helpful guide for those who had just lost their jobs and had no idea what the hell to do.

You've just been let go. Your career (and life) has just gone into a tailspin. What now?

Breathe
Spend some alone time if you need. Your mind is racing. Go for a walk. Hit the gym. Meditate. Do something to calm

down.

Have a good cry, if you need one

You are a human, not a robot. It's totally normal to have an overwhelming sense of fear right after you're let go. Getting your initial emotions out is important in the healing and rebuilding process. Whether you cry on a loved one's shoulder or let it all out in the shower when no one is around, it's totally okay to get out your sadness and fear.

Don't make any rash decisions

The worst decisions are made in the midst of raging emotions. Don't put your house on the market, sell your car, or take your pet to the animal shelter. Also refrain from slashing tires, sending death threats or smashing mailboxes. You're scared and overly emotional. Don't do anything out of fear, anger or stupidity. (But voodoo dolls are totally fine. Go to town!)

Tell your friends and loved ones

You may feel like you've let all of your loved ones down—particularly your spouse, partner or children. This won't be an easy conversation to have, but you need to let your close friends and loved ones know that your job situation has changed. You need to let them know because having a strong support circle will be critical in the coming days, weeks and months. Your immediate family certainly doesn't have to be the very first to know, as they are usually the hardest to face. I was terrified to tell my husband and parents. So I called a few close friends first and let it all out to them. You'll probably find that your own support group of family and friends will be overwhelmingly supportive, especially if you were miserable in your job. As a very smart lady once told me, "Bad news doesn't get better with time." So just rip it off like a Band-Aid and let them know as soon as you feel ready.

Notify your colleagues and connections

It takes an enormous amount of courage to admit to the world that you've lost your job, no matter what the situation. But unfortunately, it must be done. When you start to notify your close colleagues and connections, don't feel that you have to get into the "why." And frankly, it's no one's business but your own. A brief and simple email will suffice. Keep it somewhat upbeat, even if you don't feel like it. Here's an email template I used to notify a board I serve on after I was let go from my job.

Hello Board,

I wanted to let you know that as of today, I'm no longer with [INSERT COMPANY]. Please update my email to megan@mwmarcom.com. I am, of course, still fully committed to the Board and am excited about this new chapter in my career!

Thank you!
Megan

(For the record, I received many congratulatory replies plus a new client lead!)

Keep a schedule

As tempting as it might be, sleeping until noon serves absolutely no purpose. Don't fall in the trap of wallowing in your self-pity. Get up. Work on projects that you've been putting off. Work out. Help a neighbor plant their garden or plant one yourself. DO SOMETHING (and binging on Netflix doesn't count). Just because you don't have a job at the current moment doesn't mean you can't contribute somehow to your home, your community or to others. Just keep going somehow, some way to keep your mind occupied.

These may sound like very no-brainer things to do but guess what? You're most likely not in the best mindset right now. These steps are simple, yet they are critical to begin the healing process. And speaking of the healing process, these crazy emotions that you're wrestling with aren't just going to go away on their own. In the next chapter, you'll read about how I dealt with the emotional implications of job loss and why it's critical to get back in the right mindset.

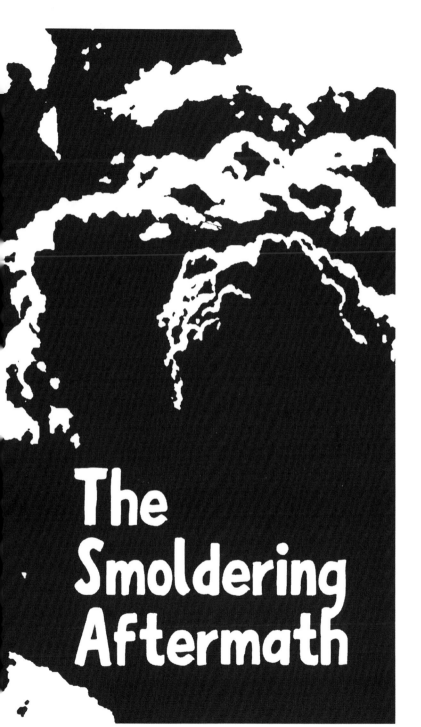

The Smoldering Aftermath

Chapter 2
The Smoldering Aftermath

"Sometimes life's going to hit you in the head with a brick. Don't lose faith."
—Steve Jobs

You are probably feeling a million things or nothing at all right now. Shock. Relief. Anger. Happiness. Terror. We, as humans, are not meant to be or act like robots. We all have real emotions that need to break through to the surface in order to start the healing process. No matter if you loved the job or just enjoyed your co-workers' company and friendship, you will undoubtedly go through a grieving process. Everyone has such different coping mechanisms. In this chapter, you'll read about my experience in getting my emotions in check and why it's critical that you do, too.

For me, I struggled with the emotional rollercoaster of rejection, lack of confidence and anxiety. Right after I lost my job, I felt an overwhelming sense of relief. I was leaving a toxic environment that was bringing out the worst in me. After the initial shock wore off, that comfort of relief felt more like a heavy badge of failure. During the first few months after I lost my job, I would wake up first thing in the morning with a panicked sort of anxiety. Where will I find work? Should I launch my own business? How will we pay bills? I'm not going to lie—it was awful. My anxiety would eventually subside throughout the day but then the cycle started all over again with the next morning's sunrise.

But at the same time, I also felt a sense of optimism. I was no longer in a negative work environment. I had the power to take my career in any direction I wanted to. "The world is your oyster," as one very wise friend put it. While that sounded all well and good, oysters certainly don't pay the mortgage, but in the grand scheme of things, he was right.

When I sat down and chatted with Jason Mollica, he described his first few days after being let go, which were very different from my own experience.

"It actually started a few hours after getting let go," he explained. "It was the support I received from my wife and my family. I never had the feeling of guilt that I let down anyone. There was encouragement from my wife in believing that I could now break out on my own."

Trying to soothe the burn

What I found after I lost my job was that dealing with the emotional aftermath was the most challenging part of the whole experience. Being let go from your job is one of the most stressful life events that we, as humans, encounter. And each individual copes very differently, much as we do when we experience the death of a loved one. We don't necessarily grieve the loss of our time in the actual role in the company or even the company itself. We end up grieving the end of a chapter in our lives, the (temporary) end of financial stability, and sometimes the end of tight-knit professional friendships. We can even grieve for our professional reputations, as we fear that a name that we've built for ourselves may in some way, shape or form be discredited or tarnished, because we weren't worthy enough to be kept around. The sting of rejection can be crippling.

Our jobs, to a certain extent, become part of our identity. Think about the last time you went to a party or event where you met new people. What's one of the first questions they ask you? "Oh, so what do you do for a living?" It's embarrassing and uncomfortable to not be able to come up with an answer.

After surveying individuals who had experienced job loss, the top three emotions that they were coping with at that time were anger, fear and anxiety. The life aspect they were most concerned about was financial stability, followed by having a career setback and loss of benefits. When asked what their fear level was at that time, on a scale of 1 through 5, their average was a 2.8.

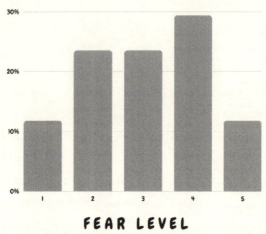

FEAR LEVEL
(1=Not fearful at all; 5 = The most fearful I've ever been)

Neglecting #1 is a big, fat ZERO

Your mental health is just as important as your physical health. This sudden life change can be frightening but not as frightening as not dealing with your emotions. Bottling everything you're feeling inside for an extended amount of time can lead to some scary stuff like compounding mental health issues and the inability to move forward. Neglecting your emotions can also have an adverse effect on your relationships, physical health and the lives of your family. You may not *feel* like getting out of bed. Get up anyway, even if it's to get a cup of coffee. You may not *feel* like going to that family birthday party. Go anyway to be surrounded by people who love and support you. You may not *feel* like going on a walk. Go anyway to get some fresh air. You can't evolve and grow if you refuse to do something different.

Things you can do to cope

Everyone deals with loss or rejection very differently. My coping mechanism was to exercise outdoors. There is a wonderful walking and biking trail in our town that I had never really had taken the time to check out. After one particularly tough day, I hopped in the car and made the five-minute drive to this beautiful trail that had once been a railway that transported passengers across Upstate New York. I was stunned to find how gorgeous and incredibly refreshing this place was. All this time, it had been only minutes from my home and I never bothered to explore what was right in front of me. After an invigorating four-mile power walk surrounded by lush, verdant trees, bright, indigo skies and crisp, fresh air, my head was cleared and mood was drastically altered. I made this zen-filled trek part of my routine for the next few months.

That one, small effort turned into a summer filled with many trail walks. I lost some of the excessive stress baggage that was hanging around my waist and was able to clear my head anytime I had a rough day. I also discovered a free Zumba class, put on by our local YMCA at a nearby town park, that was another way for me to get out, get some fresh air and work up a sweat. It was the best therapy I never had to pay for. I was around really excited and energetic people who were moving and grooving and laughing and having a great time. How could that not be contagious? I slowly was able to come out of my "hide-under-a-rock-all-day" funk and became super excited about my life and career again.

Even doing something as simple as going for a

five-minute walk can greatly alter your mood. Although most people don't love going to the gym, the mental benefits exercise gives us are second to none. The Mayo Clinic tells us that exercise has many stress-busting benefits such as pumping up endorphins, improving our mood and acting as sort of meditation in motion to distract you from the day's worries.

Making sure you have a healthy coping mechanism is critical for the healing and rebuilding process. And in turn, if you don't heal, you can't move forward to seek out new opportunities. But it takes finding purpose again to kick off the process.

Many times we are completely caught up in our own drama, sorrow, depression, troubles, etc., that we don't see the human struggle in others. When we give our time and talents to others, we then find purpose. According to the Corporation for National and Community Service, volunteering boosts pride and satisfaction in someone's work, establishes a renewed sense of accomplishment, and helps individuals solve problems, strengthen communities and connect to others. Finding a way to serve a greater purpose, other than your own, can help put your situation into perspective.

Getting all of the negative energy off of your chest is also extremely important. Whether you choose to talk to a friend or someone who's gone through job loss, it's important that you have an outlet to express what you're feeling. I was very fortunate to have a few close friends who were in the same boat as I was in when they lost their job. Their wisdom, care and concern were invaluable and helped me through a tough time. Therapy is also a great option, especially if you left a particularly traumatic or depressing job. If you don't feel comfortable talking to someone, then writing down what you're feeling is a great way to rid yourself of any negative feelings.

Lastly, just because someone ruined your day (or week ... or month), doesn't mean that you're the only one who needs to catch a break. If you want to put some good karma out in the world, perform a random act of kindness. There is so much hatred and negativity out in the world, so put some good karma out there and do something nice for a random stranger or even a neighbor or friend. The best part is, they won't even expect it!

And even better, performing a random act of kindness will help you to naturally de-stress. In a study published in *Clinical Psychological Science*, researchers discovered that helping others reduces the impact of stress on a person's health. They found that individuals who performed more acts of kindness throughout the day were less likely to exhibit negative emotions. They were also able to maintain their positive emotions. However, during the days in which they did not perform kind acts, the participants reported a decrease in positive emotions in response to daily stressors.

The key is to take care of yourself mentally and physically now so that when the next opportunity comes your way, you'll be diving in with a clear mind and body.

Everyone copes with this highly stressful time in different ways. Whether it's through prayer, meditation, the support of family and friends, or by taking a stab at a voodoo doll, channeling your negative emotions in a healthy way is critical in order to move forward. In the next chapter, you'll hear from other job loss survivors and how they coped with their emotions in the weeks and months following their job loss.

* * *

The fact of the matter is, you are not the first one to lose your job and you certainly won't be the last. Here are stories from individuals who have been through job loss and how they coped with their emotions afterwards. I hope when you read these accounts, that you draw hope, inspiration, understanding, and perhaps humor, when you hear their tales of job loss. Their stories may be completely different or eerily similar to your own. Read about how others, in your same shoes, coped with the emotional impact of their job loss.

"Through prayer and reflection. I understood that this was just another part of my life's journey and was ready to see where I would land next."

"I started a small company to buffer my finances, caring for my daughter is my motivation to keep striving to earn an income."

"At first I was positive. It was such a relief getting out of a bad situation. I was happy to be able to start fresh. But I was also sad because I felt like a failure ending up being forced to leave. After a while I realized that finding a new job was not that easy. Especially since my previous employer told people not to hire me. In the end, I went and got a coach to help me move forward."

"I once read that the best revenge was "Wild Success." So ... rather than worry about what happened, I got busy immediately redesigning my life. I started my own business as a writer. We are living off savings as I write this. We are also preparing to sell our house and move so we can look for jobs elsewhere. I will continue to write part time. (My hopes are that I can work as a writer, speaker and consultant and not need to find a job, but for now ... a job seems necessary.) Since I taught leadership and optimism, now is my time to use what I know."

"I didn't—I buried myself in work. Not a healthy coping mechanism."

"Having a strong circle of friends helped immensely."

"I buried myself in home projects and working on a photography project so I didn't think about it much. I secretly wished the company would go under."

"I spoke to my family and attorney."

"I worked out, prayed, talked to friends and family, listened to past experiences of those who had been through job loss."

"Got another job right away."

"Held my head high and knew it wasn't me, it was them. They lost a hard working employee!"

"I dove into my new business and tried to use the emotion as inspiration. It wasn't always easy. But, as the years went on, I found that getting let go helped me become a better person. Not one defined by the office I worked for."

"I took the time to decompress and figure out what I wanted next. I joined a program for entrepreneurs and got some coaching to help me find direction."

"I tried to stay busy. I used my full time job to pay my bills and to pay rent on a retail location that I was renting for my store. Plus, I had a part time weekend job. My biggest worry was trying to make sure my bills and rent for retail store were paid. Looking for a job is filled with rejection and hits to self-confidence. It helped to be busy so I had something to focus on besides the job search."

"It was what it was. I was worried about the future, but decided to give myself a month before looking for another job."

"I had a marital breakdown on my mind so the job loss was the least of it. I soon realized what a great opportunity it was—a ton of redundancy pay and total freedom where I went next."

"I leaned on family and friends and also my colleagues that were let go at the same time. We became a support system for each other. A lifeline!"

As you can see, everyone grieves the loss of their job and handles the emotions very differently. This can be a very trying time for you emotionally as no one likes to feel like a failure. But taking steps to ensure that your head is in the right place is critical to move forward and build a new career. In the next chapter, you'll learn about healthy ways you can channel your negative emotions, relieve stress and anxiety and grasp a positive outlook on life again.

* * *

Feeling a little down and out, anxious, sad, or frightened? Congratulations—you're human! Everyone has bad days, especially after you've gotten the boot from your job. In order to start rebuilding your career, it's a good idea to address and channel any emotional distress that weighs on you. Below are a few things you can do to get back in the right mindset.

Talk to someone

This one is probably the most difficult thing to do. You are basically saying out loud that you are unemployed. But talking out your anger, sadness, fear, anxiety or anything else you're feeling can be far more helpful than you can imagine. Don't be afraid to rely on your family and friends during this uncertain time. There's a free site called 7cups.com that connects you to trained listeners, if you don't want to enlist the help of a friend. Or if you don't feel comfortable talking to them, you can always seek council in a professional therapist or religious leader.

Write it down

Keeping a journal of your emotions is a healthy way to get negative energy off of your chest. Even if you write for only five minutes per day, you'll feel five times better than what you did before. Journaling has amazing mental and psychological benefits. According to an article published on psychcentral.com, journaling helps clarify your thoughts and feelings by getting in touch with your internal self, allows you to know yourself better by evaluating situations and people who are toxic for your emotional well-being, reduces stress by releasing the intensity of emotional feelings, and solves problems more effectively by unlocking creative capabilities.

Exercise

Now I'm the first to admit that I'm no Jillian Michaels and don't really like to work out. But after I lost my job, I knew I needed to get out and get moving to get myself in a much better place physically (and mentally). My husband and I discovered a walking and biking trail in my town and we loved going to walk it almost every night. I also took advantage of a free yoga class at a local park which was so much fun. Exercising out in nature is so refreshing (and free!) and is the perfect prescription for clearing your head and keeping your physical and mental health in check.

Start with baby steps if you're not used to exercising a lot. Find something that seems fun or enjoyable to you. The worst thing you can do is start off your regime doing something you hate, like running is for me. Go on a twenty-minute walk and work your way up. Try a free community exercise class, like Zumba or Yoga. Dance it out to JT's new jam. Or you can go the unconventional route like rock climbing, kayaking or hiking. Just get up and move every day (or every other day). Your body, your mind and the universe will all thank you.

Volunteer

This is the single best thing you can do to put good karma into the world. Your emotional healing won't start until you take the "you" out of it. Think about how you can use your talents to help an organization in need. If enjoy cooking, try preparing meals at a soup kitchen. If you love animals, help out at an animal shelter or take in a foster pet. If you enjoy being outside, take part in a community clean up day. There are a million things you can do to help others or our planet.

Just start with one act of volunteerism. You'll feel great about your good deed and chances are, will want to help out again. Try a few different organizations to see which is the most enjoyable for you. Another benefit of volunteering is that you never know who you'll meet. Maybe you'll come across a new friend, a potential job lead or a new client. Fate has an interesting way of connecting people for the good.

Perform a Random Act of Kindness

You may feel enormously wronged, down or your luck and that the world is against you. But remember, that other people in this world are hurting along with you, sometime facing much more daunting scenarios than you. Random acts of kindness take as little as thirty seconds to perform, can cost nothing to do and drastically change someone's day.

You can set a goal of performing one random act of kindness per week and work your way up. Brush the snow off the car parked next to you. Bring your neighbor some fresh cut flowers from your garden. Help that person struggling to get their groceries in their vehicle. Not only will it make their day, but you'll feel great about helping someone out and forget why you were having a bad day.

The only constant in life is change.

You may feel the weight of the world on your shoulders and that your life is ruined. That's certainly not the case. You will not be in this situation forever so just try to decompress and clear your head. Just remember, you will not be in this same place in one year or even six months! Just try to keep that notion in mind and keep the faith.

Now that you're on your way to getting a handle on your emotions, it's time to start rebuilding your career. Before diving head first into a new venture, there are some things you need to consider before launching off the diving board. In the next chapter, you'll learn about steps you need to take post-job loss to get your finances in order, career materials updated and the new transition starting smoothly!

* * *

Chapter 3
Extinguishing the Flames

"It's supposed to be hard. If it wasn't hard, everyone would do it.
The hard ... is what makes it great."
–Jimmy Dugan, *A League of Their Own*

Now that you've taken some time to regroup and clear your head, it's time to get to work to find your purpose and construct a future career plan. Anytime change is needed, the most necessary thing to do is take steps *forward*, no matter how big or little those steps may be. In this chapter, we'll talk about what you need to do to get any loose ends tied up, updating your career materials, getting your personal finances in order and using your existing network of connections to get back up on your feet again.

You're starting with a blank slate. This can be a very exciting time for you! You could take your career path in so many directions. Your head may be racing with a million different ideas. Have you always wanted to start your own business? Thought about getting into an entirely different career field? Have you dreamed about going back to school and getting that degree you always wanted? How about backpacking through Europe or becoming a bartender in Saint Thomas?

Whoa, Nelly! Your head may be racing with anticipation. Before you make any big decisions, there are some clean-up items you need to do first to close out your former career and start blazing the path to your new life chapter.

For some people, this part may not be easy to get through. Putting a final closure to your last position after your job loss aftermath may be as difficult as the actual job loss itself. The reason it's so difficult is because you are essentially admitting to the world that you've lost your job. You may not care at all (good for you!) or this might be a scary thing for you.

For me, this was definitely one of the most uncomfortable experiences in my job loss journey. But it was also the most exciting. I had so many possibilities as to what I could do and where I could take my career (you'll hear more about it in the next chapter). I lived by the belief that I would have an open mind to every opportunity that presented itself to me no matter what it was. But I knew that I needed to put a closure on the old chapter so I could move forward with the new one.

I found that the easiest way to go about this was knowing that I *had* to hit the reset button. You have to muster up the courage to do this before you can move forward and have the career you've always wanted. So I put on my big girl pants and checked off each item one by one. And guess what? Nothing bad happened! I didn't spontaneously combust. I didn't lose touch with my friends or connections. My dog didn't run away (he knows he's got it made in the shade). Life just rolled on one day at a time.

And you too will see that there's nothing to worry about and there's no shame in hitting the reset button.

Jason Mollica explained that it was the support of his family that had the greatest impact on his new chapter.

"The easiest part was actually getting support from my community of friends, both in person and online. A group of colleagues actually got together and made a blog post of support a few days after I was let go from my job. It not only touched me deeply, it showed that if you are honest about who you are and believe in what you are doing, people will support you. I will always be grateful for that."

A brand new you

No matter what path you decide to pursue next or what path you are merely thinking about pursuing, a current rundown of where you've been and what talents you're bringing with you will be important. Maybe you haven't updated your resume in a really long time or don't even have one at all. Now's the time to get that task tackled! A resume is your very own customized accomplishments document. Of course you'll want to include your past work experience with dates and responsibilities but you should also consider including other accomplishments, awards and extracurricular activities. You might think that they may not mean a whole lot but to someone reviewing your resume, they may seem very impressive! For example, I include organizations I'm involved with, past work award nominations, and other items of recognition. You never know what bit of information may make an instant connection.

If you're unsure about how to either create a resume or what to include, I've included some great sites in the resources section at the end of the book. Or ask a professionally-minded friend for help. Make sure your information on all of your social media sites, such as LinkedIn, is updated to indicate that you're no longer at your old position. You certainly don't want a business contact calling your old place of employment only to find out you're not there anymore—that happened to me! Cleaning up your digital presence may also set off new opportunities when your network is notified you're no longer at your job—the one time those pesky LinkedIn notifications can help!

I had a contact reach out to me after seeing I was no longer at my old job. She asked if I was looking for something new and referred me to a job opening. You just never know. In my job loss journey, I also met with a recruiter to see what full-time opportunities were out there, while I was launching my business. She was very helpful and gave me excellent recommendations that helped to beef up my resume. She also connected me with an organization that was hiring for a director of communications position. It turned out the position wasn't a good fit for me but having that connection was a foot in the door for other opportunities.

It's all about the Benjamins, baby
One of the most important things you can do at this

stage of job loss is to get your financial affairs in order. Every single person has financial commitments that don't just stop because you've found yourself out of work and out of a paycheck. Mortgages, student loans, car payments—the list goes on and on! In a survey I conducted for this book from individuals who had experienced job loss, the life aspect they were most concerned about right after they had lost their jobs was financial stability. This is a completely understandable thing to be nervous about since no one wants the bill collector to come showing up at your door or the electricity shut off at your house! Money is a very easy thing to get freaked out about—especially when the cash flow has stopped, or will stop soon.

But there are ways you can mitigate these anxieties for the time being. You can start by going through your monthly expenses and see what can stay and what needs to go. For me, my husband and I really had to prioritize our expenses in a way that was friendly with our bank account yet still allowed us to be free from a lot of restriction. The one expense I did have to give up was having someone to clean my house. It was a little necessary gift to myself since my husband travels a great deal for his job and I'm usually responsible for many of the responsibilities around the house. I hated letting our cleaning lady go (see the domino effect?) but I knew it had to be done for the time being to save some cash. It's a fine but necessary line to balance but in the end, if you can trim back your excess expenses, it will help your bottom line (and ease your anxieties) over the course of your career transition.

If you were involuntarily let go from your job, you will most likely qualify for unemployment. Different people have different views on taking unemployment but here's one essential fact. <u>You have paid into the program and are entitled to that benefit.</u> So why not use those extra funds to help alleviate some of your financial stress? That's money you can put toward necessary expenses such as your mortgage, rent, car payment, student loans, or utility bills. The process to draw unemployment varies state-to-state, so start the application process by researching your state's policies and procedures for the unemployment application process. Every state is different so make sure you find the solution that is applicable to your situation. For example, if you received severance like I did, you might need to wait to file until your (take out weekly) pay expires (I'm not sure everyone is on a weekly schedule).

Jason Mollica explains that when he applied for unemployment, it was game changer for him.

"The most difficult thing I've dealt with actually applying for unemployment." Jason went on to explain, "It was incredibly humbling. If you want your pride to get swallowed, walk into an unemployment office. I wasn't long without a 'job,' but those initial weeks were difficult."

Jody adds that the best companies will help provide resources for the person losing their job.

"We've usually given them recommendations as to what to do next. I've always made sure that I'm prepared," she says. "I give them info on what to do, such as how to file unemployment, and send them to a career counselor to help with their resume and help pick you up off your feet. A good company will do that."

Still have anxiety over money? Guess what—that's being human and is completely normal! If you still need some help figuring it all out, there are plenty of free online tools that can help you figure out all of the dollars and cents of job loss. Or if you feel more comfortable talking with a real human, get a recommendation for a financial planner. They can help you set a path during your career transition. Also, don't ever be too prideful to ask for help if times are tough. After I lost my job, each of our mothers told us (without having to ask) that if we needed some extra cash to get by, we were to let them know. And there is certainly no shame in asking for help, when it's truly needed. Fortunately, that wasn't the case and we didn't need to go that route but had we gotten behind on mortgage payments, electric bills or any other necessary expense, it was nice to know that we had a back up.

Spreading your web of connections

If you've got an idea of what you want do when you grow up (ha!) then you'll need to do some research and make some new contacts. That's right. I'm talking about networking! Networking doesn't have to be a chore. You may immediately think of a bunch of shy people in stuffy suits picking at the appetizer selection of cubed cheese and vegetables and avoiding eye contact with everyone.

But not all networking events paint this bland picture. I've attended many really great events at breweries, newly opened historic spaces and new local eateries. You've got to remember, even if meeting new people is difficult for you, opening yourself to new people and experiences is a critical step in your journey to the career and passions you want to pursue. If you stay in the same circle with the same people and same experiences, absolutely nothing will change.

So what's the goal with networking? What are you looking to accomplish? It can be literally anything that can put you on the track that you want to hop on. The key to successful networking is getting involved with business and professional groups that you find fun, different and interesting. They can also be targeted to your specific industry. Business-focused groups, such as chambers of commerce or rotary groups, can open you up to a wide variety of potential resources.

By joining my local chamber, I was able to make many potential client contacts that I wouldn't have ordinarily made. Or there are groups that are more industry-specific, such as an advertising club or a technology group. Individuals in those types of groups most likely have a ton of collective experience and can be invaluable resources. Getting feedback, advice and guidance from people in the industry you either currently are in or want do get into is really important. Chances are, these connections won't sugarcoat the state of the industry, which is a good thing. With any next step, it's important that you take it with eyes wide open.

You can also discover new connections through your existing network. In the survey I conducted for this book, the number one action that respondents took after they had lost their job was to reach out to existing connections for new opportunity recommendations—hence, the importance of keeping your contacts in the loop! I'll never forget a woman whom I worked with at the job I was let go from. We weren't best friends by any means but worked well together and had respect for each other. A few days had passed after my departure from the company and I received a message from her on LinkedIn. She sent me the nicest note saying how shocked she was that I had been let go, wished me all the best and sent a job opening she had come across online. Talk about unexpected! Your connections can not only be a true blessing, but also a critical launching catalyst for the next phase of your career.

Can't Stop, Won't Stop

At this stage in your job loss journey, it's important to set goals for the new chapter in your life. Goals serve three purposes—they keep you moving forward; they give you a sense of purpose when working towards something; and they increase self-confidence when those set goals are achieved. Your goals should be specific, measurable, attainable, realistic, and timely—or as we like to call them in the marketing world, SMART goals. You don't have to start with a huge goal, just one or two small goals. For example, if you want to network with people in your industry of interest, a SMART goal may look like this:

Reach out to eight industry-leaders to request a coffee meeting in a one-month period

Attend three networking events in a two-month time period.

As you achieve more and more goals, stretch yourself and make them a little bigger each time. Stretch yourself. If you don't achieve them on the first go-round, that's okay! The important point is that you tried—and you're so much farther than you were if you hadn't tried at all. Didn't hit your goal? Keep trying and don't give up.

Tying up loose ends like updating your resume, reaching out to your connections, making new contacts, getting your personal finances in order is the first stepping stone to create the career you want. Now that you've got an idea about what you need to do to move forward, hear about what other job loss survivors and what they did to springboard off to a new career in the next chapter!

* * *

These individual stories aren't meant to be used as comparison to your own situation, but rather to serve as an inspiration and a reminder that you are not alone in this transition. I hope these testimonials and experiences will show that more people than you know understand what you're going through. In this section, read about how other job loss survivors got back up on their feet to reinvent themselves in their careers!

"Started working on projects and business ventures that I had not been able to focus on prior due to my job. I saw the lay off as a huge gift to 'get off my butt' and do what I love to do."

"Prayer."

"With the help of my coach. Finding out what my goals were, I had forgotten ... I did a lot of inner work that helped me see myself as worthy regardless of my achievements."

"I immediately started writing articles and transitioned to books. I have four books on Amazon now! I looked for positive feedback to reinforce my efforts. I also created a YouTube channel that now has fifty videos on it. I get about 500 views per month. I also dove into many positive books in order to channel my emotions is a more positive way. I joined a weekly Bible study and turned all this over to God. According to Proverbs, all success comes from God."

"Eventually, I did find a new path, but it took years."

"While I don't know if I will return to the workforce, I'm confident I excelled at my job. Should I decide to return to work, I'll bring this confidence with me."

"I haven't, really. I now work in a totally different field and am terrified to go back to working in my original field."

"I joined an outplacement company."

"I looked at videos on YouTube about being unemployed, listen to past experiences of people that lost their jobs and were they're now."

"I don't think I ever lost confidence. I always knew I would land on my feet because I had skills. I don't think I thought I would be without a job so long the second time, but I ended up doing pretty well."

"Within a few weeks I had a job offer because of my connections. They knew me and how well I can pull things together and run with them."

"It wasn't easy. I rode my adrenaline for a long period of time. However, having my own business opened my eyes to the opportunities that were now out there for me. As the days went on, I felt more and more confident."

"Meditation and prayer, gratitude, focusing on the good things in life and my previous accomplishments. Friends and family. I got a decent package so had lots of time to not worry about finances."

"It was hard. I avoided people I used to work with because I felt embarrassed and that they were judging me. It made me work twice as hard at my next job."

"Re-working my resume helped me realize all of my skills."

"I was on a high with the redundancy money and quickly found better work."

"By going on interviews and by talking to previous employers who serve as references for me. They encouraged me and also reminded me that I was a talented professional with passion and integrity. Unfortunately, the leadership at the job I lost really pushed me down rather than encouraged me, so it was for the best I was no longer there anyway."

Hopefully you've gained some inspiration from these job loss survivors and can incorporate some of their tactics into your own career-rebuilding plan. Now that you've got a good idea of the direction you need to start down, the next section will offer some more detailed steps to hit the reset button on your career!

* * *

So you're back up on your feet and are ready to hit the reset button on your career. Wonderful! This is the springboard to your new career life. In this section, we'll give you some more specific things you need to do to launch your career-rebuilding plan, from updating your resume to getting your finances in order to building your contact list.

Refresh your resume

Everyone needs an updated resume, whether you've had one your whole career or have never had such a thing. This is a chance for you to showcase your newly refreshed skills, talents and experiences. Here are my top tips for constructing your new and improved resume:

The design is just as important, if not more important, than the content itself. Your resume needs to stand out in a stack of possibly hundreds.

Stick to only two fonts types—a serif font for the heading and a sans serif font for the body. Serif fonts include details or small decorative flourishes on the ends of some of the strokes that make up characters. An example would be the Times New Roman font. Sans serif fonts don't have these details or flourishes. An example would be the Arial font.

Don't be afraid to use a little pop of color or graphical elements such as icons, but don't go overboard!

Make sure the typeface is legible for anyone to read. You shouldn't go any smaller that 10pt font.

If you're still unsure about design, there are several online marketplaces that will very inexpensively design and format your new resume. See the Resource section for a list of websites.

Hyperlink items such as email and personal website (if you choose to share it). And to take it a step further, since we're living in a mobile world, you can even include a link set to dial your phone number.

Highlight your accomplishments no matter how big or small they may be to you.

Keep your resume to no more than two pages as a rule of thumb.

Write clearly and concisely. Humans today now have the attention span of a goldfish (a short eight seconds!) so more times than not, your resume will be scanned over quickly. Make sure the reader will get a clear picture of who you are as a professional in a brief amount of time.

Highlight your most recent accomplishments first. The job you had at Chili's as a waitress ten years ago probably isn't relevant, unless you're going in to the food service industry. Really dial in your priorities and polish up the duty descriptions that coincide.

List all organizations you are a part of both professionally and personally. Showing that you have interests outside of your career will demonstrate that you're a well-rounded person. Also, be sure to list extra committees that you've served on or special projects that you've helped with.

Proofread, proofread, proofread. Our brains are technically not wired to self-edit, unless we put away our handiwork after a day or two. Have a trusted friend or contact who's got an eagle eye for grammar and spelling look over your work.

Don't over exaggerate or blatantly lie. Number one, it's not cool. Number two, it will destroy your credibility if you get caught. Number three, it's dumb. Really dumb. So just don't do it to begin with.

And some helpful advice from our favorite HR pro, Jody?

"I always tell everyone that the purpose of a resume is only to get the interview," she explains. "You're the one who's going to be getting the job and proving 'I'm the right person for this job.' You can go in to all the details when you get the interview. So you don't need to have fourteen pages with fifteen bullets—hit the ones that are the most important that really showcase who you are as a professional."

Update your LinkedIn profile

Making sure your online contacts know you've moved on to greener pastures is an important step to close out this career chapter. This might be a difficult step to accomplish because it's right there in black and white that your employment has ended with your former company. And it's also out there to the world no less. But, think of this as an online reset button! Just like your resume, you should give your LinkedIn profile a refresher as well—and if you don't have one, now's the time to make it happen!

Here are a few LinkedIn tips to take into consideration, in addition to the resume tips above:

Search suggested connections and invite individuals who

you know to connect.

Include interactive media, such as video or web links, to any relevant work you've created.

Ask your contacts to post recommendations to your page.

Apply for Unemployment

Start by researching your state's policies and procedures for the unemployment application process. This is additional funding that you are entitled to as a taxpayer. You've paid into those benefits and they are yours to take advantage of. Whether you need the funds to cover necessary bills, rent or mortgage payments or any other financial commitments, any additional income that you can get during this transition period will only help you sleep better at night!

Meet with a Financial Planner

Get your finances up to snuff by meeting with a financial planner. They'll walk you through a financial road map that will help ease your money anxiety and put you on a fiscally responsible path. You can do some leg work ahead of time and make the process a bit easier by writing down all of your current monthly expenses such as rent or mortgage, car payments, student loans, utilities, childcare, internet, groceries, etc. Then, select expenses that you can *realistically* eliminate for the time being.

Join Networking Groups

Research a few local networking groups relevant to your

industry or the industry you want to break into. Most groups let you attend their upcoming events for free so you can test the waters, meet some current members and see if it's a good fit. Once you do some research, choose two or three groups that you feel would be beneficial to get involved with. I throw out the numbers two or three because any more than that will leave you feeling overextended and overwhelmed.

To take it a step further, become active in those groups once you confirm it's a good fit for you. Do you know how to throw a killer event? Do you enjoy raising funds for a great cause? Offer your skills and talents to that organization. I've served in various marketing and PR capacities for groups I've been involved with other the years. The experience has not only helped me meet new people but it's an additional skill you can add to your resume.

Start a Blog

Blogging is one of the best and easiest ways to start building credibility and influence in your respective industry. Everyone should have an opinion, no matter what field you're in. Blogging is a method that has brought countless leads to those who actively write on topics of their choice. Blogs are typically 400–600 words and incorporate images, video and other engaging visuals. The platform I highly recommend is Medium. It's a simple, easy-to-use platform that was built specifically for writers, and is free to use!

Reach out to existing contacts

A very wise connection of mine once told me that your friends, colleagues and existing contacts are the best sources of referrals you can find. **So go through your contact list, LinkedIn connections and reach out to ten people.** Let them know that you're making a career change and ask them if they could help you out with whatever it is you're looking to accomplish. This could be a job opening, sales lead, investment opportunity or just some good advice.

Meet with a Career Coach or Recruiter

Whether or not you want to stay in your industry, a career coach or recruiter can give you some really handy advice and guide you down the right path regarding your career. They will be able to tell you what opportunities are out there, historical industry trends they've seen and can review your resume to make sure your skills fit the criteria. A recruiter might also be able to match your skills with a current job opening and submit your resume to their clients who are looking to fill a position. The best part is, there is most likely no cost to you to meet with a recruiter, as their fees are paid by the company looking to hire.

Set Your SMART Goals

Remember, SMART goals are specific, measurable, attainable, realistic, and timely. Start by setting three small goals and build from there. Spend thirty to sixty minutes every day on your goals, or longer if you'd like! Do this consistently and preferably in the morning, when your mental gas tank is full. Need some visual inspiration? Create a vision board with photos and words of the thing you're looking to achieve as a positive reminder of what you're working for!

You've got a plan—now it's time to get to work! Getting your finances in order, resume refreshed, blog up and going, and networks growing (and then some!) will help put you on the path toward the career of your dreams. So what is that career exactly? In the next chapter, you'll read about my career renaissance and how you can find what career path is your calling.

* * *

Igniting Your Passions

Chapter 4
Igniting Your Passions

> "It's a new dawn, it's a new day, it's a new life for me."
> —Michael Buble

You're now standing at a precipice of opportunity. Your old career life is behind you. A new path of promise lies before you. Which course will life take you on? How will you surprise yourself in another one, three or five years? What new experiences will you have? What new places will you see or how many new friends will you make? Most importantly, you'll probably ask yourself, "What was I so worried about?" In this chapter, you'll hear my career renaissance story and how your curiosities can lead to potential uncovered paths you didn't even know existed.

I was very fortunate and decided to start my own business about six months prior to losing my job. From the time I graduated with my undergrad, I always wanted to start my own marketing consulting business. My dad is a small business owner so I practically grew up in his independent insurance office from the time I was born. I'm pretty sure I was one of the few four-year-olds that had their own desk! I not only saw how hard he worked, but also the flexibility he gained by being the boss and the kindness and appreciation he showed to those who worked for him. Witnessing my dad's example had a huge impact on how I wanted to be as professional and a boss.

So about seven years ago, I started a side-hustle and landed my very first marketing client for a small startup (all while keeping my full-time job). I was psyched! I was finally pursuing my dream of self-employment. Except that it turned into a disaster. The client was unfocused, disorganized and failed to pay me in a reasonable amount of time. I literally almost had to take her to small claims court to get the mere $500 she owed me. Needless to say, I really questioned whether or not this is what I wanted to do. Were all clients this way? Did I really have what it took to make this work?

Slowly, I turned my attention elsewhere. I enrolled in grad school at St. Bonaventure University in 2011 (again, while working full time!), which turned out to be one of the best decisions I ever made. Really creative, smart and fun classmates and professors surrounded me, and I thrived in that environment. I tell people, after my very first class, I felt dumber and smarter all at the same time. Dumber because I should have known this stuff to begin with and smarter because I now know it. In the midst of all of the papers, classes, projects and deadlines, the dream of owning my own business still lingered but the timing wasn't right yet. Sixteen months later, I graduated at the top of my class and earned an award for my final thesis. But more importantly, I came away with a whole new set of knowledge I never had before. It was amazing.

Fast-forward another two years to 2013. The program director of my master's program reached out and was looking for alumni of the program to serve as adjunct professors and thought I would be a great fit because of my success in the program. Me? A professor? Whoa. Teaching at the college level had never, ever been on my radar but I jumped at the chance to try something new! I was terrified when I showed up to my first class, with seventeen sets of judgmental eyes staring at me. But I put on my poker face, got through it and to this day, I'm still a part of the adjunct staff and continue to teach and mentor some fantastic students that go through the master's program every year.

I had been at my full-time job since 2010, all while going to school and teaching on an adjunct basis. About two years before I was let go, I could see and feel a change in the company I worked for—and not a good one. I had been applying for new jobs for quite some time because I was terrified to pursue my consulting business, but jobs in my fields and at my level were few and far between and sought a lot of demand in the market. Knowing I needed to face my business fear and do what I really wanted to do, I filed for my business DBA in January 2015, and planned to consult as a side job for the time being. After that, I was full steam ahead, creating a new logo, building my website and creating profiles on various marketing services sites. And just a few short months later, I signed my first client! I was so excited and knew I was on to something. After watching Michelle Ward's "How to Ditch Your Day Job" on CreativeLive, I made a decision that I wanted to give this a shot full time. I made a plan to stash away emergency savings, build more clients and eventually leave my job in March of 2016. My wonderfully supportive hubby was on board and I couldn't wait to get to work.

Then, I got the F-bomb dropped on me. It's so fascinating how the best laid out plan with the best intentions can be blown to smithereens. I have to say that when you are thrown into survival mode, resiliency becomes part of your everyday life. You spend money differently, you look at life differently, you see your relationships differently. And you absolutely refuse to give up.

Jason also brushed himself off and got to work after losing his job. He greatly relied on the expertise and guidance of his in-laws to get his business up and running.

"My in-laws were also incredibly helpful because they have been business owners for decades," he explained. "A week after my new chapter began, my father-in-law and I sat in our kitchen and I went to school. While I understood business, he gave me a better, more traditional outlook. I use many of those teachings to this day."

Jody agrees that in most cases, this abrupt life change can be all for the best. "Sometimes a termination, an elimination, whatever it may be, is the best thing in the world," she explains. "In a few months time, you're going to go 'Oh my God, I'm so happy where I am' or 'I'm so happy I'm not dealing with that.' So sometimes, it's a blessing in disguise. Just persevere. Just keep pushing through. That's all you can do."

Since being let go, I've explored passions that I never

knew were important to me and that I was good at—such as writing! A good friend of mine encouraged me to participate in NaNoWriMo—or National Novel Writing Month. I had no idea what the hell I was doing but with my friend's encouragement, I started writing a historical fiction novel that had been mustering in my mind for some time. The book is only about two-thirds of the way finished but that was two-thirds more than I had ever imagined writing. I loved the way that the story took on a life of its own in my head. It was the kind of book that I would enjoy reading.

Perhaps if I had not lost my job, I wouldn't have had the courage to start my own business and take it full time. Starting your own business is crazy scary but it's so rewarding. After I lost my job, I reached out to my only client, let him know that my time has freed up and if he had more work for me. Two weeks later, he offered me nearly full-time hours after his project manager had left. Timing is a funny thing, don't you think?

And certainly if I had not lost my job, I wouldn't be writing this book—hoping to help and guide at least one person (but hopefully many more) going though this challenging yet exciting time in their career.

Time is a finite thing. In the words of the fabulous Kasey Musgraves, "We only have so many trips around the sun." Suppressing your curiosities about subjects or art forms blocks yourself to new opportunities, experiences and connections to others. The job loss journey you're going through should be a time of self-discovery and open-mindedness.

Invest in yourself

Investing in yourself, your knowledge and your mental and emotional health is never money wasted. When I signed up for a self-publishing course at Self-Publishing School (which I highly recommend if you want to write a book), I started to feel guilty because it was more money than I would have liked to spend. But then I remembered how crummy it made me feel when my past jobs wouldn't send me to trainings or they cried poor as an excuse not to let me take a class. Now, I'm the only one responsible for myself and my continuing education so I vowed to do whatever I reasonably can to make sure I can to keep my mind and my skills sharp. So if you have a curiosity to learn about something new, it's silly to hold yourself back over money or fear. From a course on history, to an Accounting 101 class, any step you can take to expand your skill set and knowledge base will only add to the richness of your life and career.

There are several sites that provide free courses and trainings on a wide variety of topics, which I have listed in the resources section. You may even want to take it a step further and obtain a certain certification or go back to school to earn that degree you've always dreamed of! I was a non-traditional student when I received my master's degree and I have zero regrets about doing so. Your education is something that no one can ever take away from you and that you can take with you for the rest of your life.

If you are looking to go back to school, there are a few

bits of advice I'd love to offer you. Earn a degree that you *want* to earn, not what you *think* you should earn. When I was looking into grad schools, I researched getting an MBA, which was the hot degree to get at the time. As I was looking through the course offerings, none of them excited me. I knew right then that this wasn't the path for me, even thought was the popular way to go. Instead, I found a master's program that I was excited about. The courses were right up my alley and I had a drive and passion to learn as much as I could during my time in the program. No matter what university or college you decide to attend or what program you enroll, you're looking at a significant investment—so make sure it's one that's right for you.

Which leads me to my next bit of advice, how the heck do you pay for your tuition, books and other expenses? If you just lost your job, this is probably a big issue for you. Even though I had a full-time job at the time, I financed my education through low-rate federal student loans. There are several other loan options out there—from private loans to personal loans from loved ones. You'll just need to research the best option for you. You'll also be able to write off the student loan interest on your taxes and earn a continuing education tax credit. Hey, no one likes to be in debt, that's for sure. But view your education as you would your mortgage. It's a long-term investment that you'll eventually get your money back on.

You can also go to school for *FREE* by earning grants and scholarships. There is a wide variety of scholarship opportunities out there, many of which can be found and applied for online. The school of your choice may even offer a scholarship to your program. The university I enrolled in offered a 20 percent reduction in tuition. All I had to do was submit a formal application and write a brief essay about why I wanted to attend St. Bonaventure University. That small and simple step saved me nearly $4,000! It goes to show that putting in a little effort can save you some significant dough in the long run.

The doors that will open for you because you continued your education will truly surprise you, as it did me. For me, the amount I've earned as an adjunct has nearly paid for my entire tuition. I never once had "become a college professor" on my list of career goals. The key is being open-minded as these new experiences present themselves in your life. And if you find they're not a good fit, you're not stuck with them forever. Or, they could completely change your life.

Now that you've hopefully started networking and researching which path you want to take on your new career journey—GO FOR IT! Do you want to start a business? Great! Are you going back to school? Wonderful! Taking your career in a whole new direction? Awesome! Now. Go. Do. It. Throw yourself into your new chapter. Run, don't walk. You will probably second-guess yourself. I know I've questioned my decision to start my business many times. But in the end, you can do absolutely anything you want to do. So go do it, and don't ever look back. In the next section, we'll hear from job-loss survivors about what they've learned about themselves by going through this life challenge and also some invaluable advice they have just for you!

* * *

These job loss survivors have been through it all—and the wonderful news is that they SURVIVED. As Steve Jobs once said, "You can only connect the dots looking back, never looking forward." When asked to reflect on their job-loss experience, their stories bring hope, inspiration and encouragement to those who are going through the same situation.

What did you learn about yourself after experiencing job loss?

"No one will take care of you better than you can take care of yourself."

"I am creative in finding solutions."

"A lot! Most importantly to be honest with myself! That I am more than my achievements!"

"I really did not learn anything that I did not already know. I taught in my classes that all we do is temporary, everything has a shelf life. I knew that that current HR manager was self-important and challenging him would be career suicide. I can live with that and I would do it all over again. I believe we must choose to do what is right. We can't control the consequences, but we must be willing to live with them. My choices were to let HR harass employees unchallenged, or to stand up for what I believed."

"I learned that I had skills, and that opportunities are out there. It can be hard to extend yourself, but it's the only thing that works."

"I am a much stronger woman than I imagined myself to be."

"Change is scary, but it's worth it in the end."

"You find out who your support systems are and who cares about you."

"That I needed to be humbled."

"That I have a great deal to offer. I land on my feet. I have pretty strong contacts. I can do this by myself."

"To believe in yourself, be positive!"

"I learned that I didn't need to allow someone else to define who I could be. By opening my mind to things I never expected, I was able to succeed as person and consultant."

"I was 80 percent happy for the first few years, then coasting and never quite fitting in with bureaucrats. I learned that when I'm not happy in a situation, I need to get out a lot faster than I did."

"That I deserve to be treated with respect and dignity, and not settle for anything less."

"I actually liked working hard and being part of a cohesive team."

"I love a challenge."

"I am resilient! I also learned that I have nurtured solid relationships and that has gone a long way. I ended up being offered three jobs within three and a half weeks of losing my job. Great problem to have. I learned this was not luck this was due to my hard work."

If you could give one piece of advice for those who have recently lost their job, what would it be?

"Take a moment to look at yourself and your life. Write down ten things that you love doing and what you would love doing even if you were to never get paid. Then start looking into ways that you could turn this passion into a career or business for yourself."

"Do not give up."

"Invest in yourself to find your inner values and build your confidence. Then be honest with yourself and decide how you want to spend the rest of your life!"

"Everything is temporary and has a shelf life. Channel the negative emotions into positive pursuits. We can't control our emotions all the time. We will most likely go through the five stages of grief. We need time, so give time, time. This is just part of life and the beginning of your next hero's journey."

"Try to actually enjoy it for a bit—chances are, you've been in a stressful situation at your previous work. Go visit friends, put your feet up, write some letters. Then get out there and see what's available. If you can, approach it as if you are your own business, marketing yourself to employers. And be picky about your next job!"

"Don't look back at the closed door, reach for the new doorknob."

"Keep the faith. There is something for you out there—you just need to believe in yourself and work hard."

"You will get a job but you cannot interview when you

are still mad and angry. It will show in the interview no matter how 'good' you feel you can cover it up. Get outplacement support and counseling. You will be with likeminded people and the professionals in this group are experts in dealing with this situation."

"Don't take jobs for granted if you are there for a long time. Take care of your job like when you first started. Be grateful, if you have a problem with somebody, walk away and don't argue."

"Get out there right away and network, network, network."

"Believe in yourself and stay positive."

"It's okay to be angry, upset, and frustrated. But don't let that one experience be your Waterloo. Make it the one thing that helps you succeed. Be everything you want to be!"

"Take the time to decompress and don't let yourself feel desperate. Even if you could get another similar job with another company, is it really what makes you happy? Listen to your gut feelings. Happiness is much more important than income."

"Hang in there. Perspective is everything. Sometimes great opportunity can come from one chapter ending and another beginning."

"Take time to learn how your skills could transition into another line of work."

"Now is the time to switch direction if that has been your secret dream. Grab the opportunity the payout gives you!"

"Find a support system of others going through the same

thing at the same time. Also to not be afraid to tell your contacts and family or friends that you lost your job—nothing to be ashamed of. They say that this will happen to each of us at least once in our lifetime. Also as cliché as it sounds, another door will open and it will be a beautiful door with a shiny handle :)"

Everyone can use a little dose of encouragement, especially when you're heading into uncharted waters, right? Hopefully these little tokens of guidance will give you the courage to forge your own path and lend you the courage to get through times of uncertainly. In the next section, we will lay out a streamlined plan that will allow you to begin your new career renaissance.

* * *

You've been through the ringer, my friends—and yes, you've made it this far through the book so that definitely makes you a friend! You've endured many sleepless nights, wrestled with the weight of the unknown heard from many people who've been in your shoes. Time to get to work!

Take a non-career focused class

The fact of the matter is that you may have talents and passions that you had no idea you had. You might discover a hobby or interest that could completely change the direction of your career—or your life for that matter! If you've always wanted to learn how to paint, take a beginners painting class. If you've always wanted to learn about sewing or woodworking or welding by all means, sign up for a workshop! In each and every one of us is a curiosity that longs to learn and discover new knowledge and skills. Learning such new things can also enhance your existing career skills as well and become extremely beneficial to your mental, emotional and physical health. Taking on a new skill has also been proven to enhance your creativity. So, find a class (either in-person or online) that interests you and go for it!

Continue your career education

Education is the single most important gift you can give yourself. Whether it's tackling a single class, earning a certification or going back to earn a degree, expanding your knowledge base and skill set can only benefit you. There are some things you can do to make sure this is the right action for you to take before making a big financial commitment. Start by researching programs or certifications of interest both online and in your area. Meet with the program director if you're thinking about attending a local college or university to get a more in-depth understanding of the coursework and admission requirements. Universities and colleges often host open houses for specific programs so attending one would be a good idea to learn more about the school and program. Talk to alumni of the program and get a better feel of what doors opened for them after they completed the program and tips on how successfully complete the required coursework.

Still want to go back to school? Great! Now you just need to figure out how you're going to pay for it. You're going to want to factor in not only tuition, but books (which can get crazy expensive!) and other course fees. For example, in my final semester, I had to get five copies of my final thesis printed and bound, which came out to be close to an extra $500. Start by researching scholarship, grant and student loan options at the federal, state and university level. Make sure you're aware of the application deadlines for each form of funding, as they are all different. Take a look at your own personal finances and see if you're able to contribute on your own.

Research starting a business

I recently made a new friend at an airport bar during a layover in Baltimore on my way to Indianapolis. He owned his own finance company in North Carolina and we started trading stories about being our own boss.

"I'm really happy I made the jump," I explained. "But, it is very scary at times."

"But you know what's scarier?" he said. "Corporate America. You never know when the axe will fall."

See, he too had lost his job with a major bank after twenty years of kicking ass at one of the nation's top investment firms. Then, after a merger, his new boss (almost half his age) came in and told him that they were merging branches and that he *could* re-apply for his job for one-fifth of the salary. He told them to go f*#k themselves, hired a few members of his team, took over 100 of his clients and started his own financial planning company right across the hall from the place who tried to knock him to the bottom of the barrel.

He has since become my hero. My new, badass hero.

Becoming an entrepreneur is one of the scariest yet most liberating experiences I've ever had in my career. I've been so fortunate to have others (especially my dad) help guide me along the way. After doing your research and talking to others who are in the industry you want to break in to, it's time to get to work!

Set up a DBA, LLC or S Corp

When starting your business, you'll need to officially file your business at the local or state level. There are several designations that you can file your business under: DBA (or Doing Business As), LLC (Limited Liability Company), Partnership or S Corporation.

So what's the difference? As defined by the US Small Business Administration:

Sole Proprietorship, DBA

A sole proprietorship is the simplest and most common structure chosen to start a business. It is an unincorporated business owned and run by one individual with no distinction between the business and you, the owner. You are entitled to all profits and are responsible for all your business's debts, losses and liabilities. I started out setting up a DBA. You are taxed as an individual but your personal assets are not protected.

LLC (Limited Liability Company)

A limited liability company is a hybrid type of legal structure that provides the limited liability features of a corporation and the tax efficiencies and operational flexibility of a partnership. You are taxed as an individual but your personal assets are protected. A lawyer or legal representative is required to set up an LLC.

Partnership

A partnership is a single business where two or more people share ownership. Each partner contributes to all aspects of the business, including money, property, labor or skill. In return, each partner shares in the profits and losses of the business. There are three general types of partnership arrangements:

General Partnerships assume that profits, liability and management duties are divided equally among partners. If you opt for an unequal distribution, the percentages assigned to each partner must be documented in the partnership agreement.

Limited Partnerships (also known as a partnership with limited liability) are more complex than general partnerships. Limited partnerships allow partners to have limited liability as well as limited input with management decisions. These limits depend on the extent of each partner's investment percentage. Limited partnerships are attractive to investors of short-term projects.

Joint Ventures act as general partnership, but for only a limited period of time or for a single project. Partners in a joint venture can be recognized as an ongoing partnership if they continue the venture, but they must file as such.

S Corporation

An S Corporation (sometimes referred to as an S Corp) is a special type of corporation created through an IRS tax election. An eligible domestic corporation can avoid double taxation (once to the corporation and again to the shareholders) by electing to be treated as an S Corporation.

Seeking out a new position in the same industry

If you still absolutely love the industry that you're in and decide to seek out employment with another company, here's a prime chance to sharpen up those interviewing skills. You've scored an interview. You've got your resume ready to rock. You're looking like a million bucks. You go to your interview, start off with a fabulous conversation with the interviewer and are feeling really great about this prospect. Then, you get "the question."

Interviewer: "I noticed a gap in your employment from Company XYZ until now. Can you explain?"

You: (gulp)

You might panic at the thought of trying to explain your dismissal from your company. But no need! According to HR expert Jody Sirianni, job eliminations are far more commonplace than they were ten years ago. So the stigma of disclosing that you've lost your job isn't as magnified. She goes on to encourage transparency, as you don't want to get caught in a lie. When answering the question, keep your explanation very brief. Don't go on and on—keep it short, sweet and to the point. And most importantly, be honest! Practice your answer before you go to the interview so you can confidently explain your job loss in a clear and concise manner.

* * *

A Final Note

"Don't give up. Don't ever, ever give up."
—Coach Jimmy Valvano

Throughout my journey, I've had several people ask me that, when I look back, am I happy I lost my job.

I'm not sure "happy" is the appropriate word but grateful might be a more accurate representation. Here's why.

The anxiety, emotional rollercoaster and sleepless nights that I experienced in the days, weeks and even months after I was let go is something I'd never wish on anyone. The fear of the unknown was more than I could bear some days but something inside me told me everything would be ok.

You truly find what you're made of when your path takes a violent turn in the direction you never saw coming. It's picking yourself back up after life knocks you down. It's the universe telling you in the loudest and clearest way "You are *not* supposed to be wasting your time here." It's finding new talents and passions you ever knew you had. It's confronting your fears head on and giving them the middle finger. The wounds of disappointment, fear and rejection will eventually heal and the feelings of self-doubt will fade into the distance of the past. It's been the ultimate learning experience and has made the "wins" throughout the last year that much sweeter.

The biggest reason why I wrote this book is to help

others by sharing my experience with job loss. Let me tell you something—it sure wasn't easy. It was so emotionally challenging and sometimes uncomfortable at times for me to relive a quite scary and uncertain point in my career. But if my advice and guidance helps just one single person, then it will be totally worth it in the end. So, with that, I encourage you to pass along any advice and guidance that you have gained from your job loss journey. You certainly don't have to write a book but anytime you can pay it forward will help you earn some good karma! You can never help others enough.

The experience has made me less judgmental and helped me encompass a better understanding of someone else's professional (and personal) struggles. Now, when I hear that someone has been fired or let go, I don't make any automatic assumptions but rather feel compassion and empathy for that person, as I know first-hand what they're going through and the journey they're about to courageously embark on.

It's also been the most triumphant and courageous chapter in my story.

In the end, I'm grateful that my life and career took this path. I see life through a whole new lens and accepted that this twist was thrown in my path for a reason. As humans, we are hyper-focused on the "right now" in our lives rather than on the big picture. When you really look at your life in a holistic way, we really don't have that much to complain about. When it's all said and done, I have a one hell of a life. I have my health that I've grow to cherish in this past year. A husband and family who love me unconditionally. A home that is filled with wonderful memories and lots of laughter. Friends who I adore, admire and know I can always rely on. I have air in my lungs and clothes on my back. Sometimes it's easy to forget all of the little things that make our life worth living when we're cast in the fire of doubt, uncertainty and self-pity.

I sincerely wish you all the best on this adventure. There are times when it won't be easy to stay positive but just keep putting one foot in front of the other with your head held high.

And just remember, keep going and everything will be okay!

Acknowledgments

To my husband—you love me at my worst and cheer me on at my best. Losing my job must have scared the absolute shit out of you, but you never let on. Thank you for being my rock, my most trusted advisor and my favorite drinking buddy when things get tough. You make me a stronger, wiser and harder-working person, and I couldn't image going through this crazy rollercoaster of a life with anyone else. I love you bad.

To my parents—thank you for raising me to be independent, driven, curious and open-minded. I couldn't have done it without your support and encouragement. I love you!

To my brother, sister-in-law and niece—I love you so much and am fiercely proud of you all. Thank you for all of your love and support.

To my wonderful HFF friend, Martina, who put the littlest seed in my head that I <u>could</u> write a book. You are totally amazeballs!

To Jody and Jason—I admire you both so much for your intelligence, work ethic and well, for both being just tremendous people. Thank you for sharing your incredible wisdom for this book and more importantly, your friendship.

To the Self-Publishing School community—thank you for providing the guidance and resources to make this dream a reality. Also, a huge, huge thank you to my SPS writing buddy, Cheryl, for your constant support and wisdom. I'm so glad we got to go on this adventure together!

To all of my amazing friends who answered the call to offer me incredible advice, and give unconditional love, and support to me while I went though my job loss journey: I am so incredibly lucky to have you in my life. You know who you are—and thank you from the bottom of my heart.

About the Author

Megan Wagner is the owner and chief marketist of MW MarCom, LLC, a marketing creative agency. As an eleven-year marketing pro, she brings out her clients' "inner artist" in the areas of communications strategy, branding, public relations, digital and social media, web development, and content strategy.

Megan's also armed with a solid education from two nationally recognized universities. She's received a B.S. in Business Administration and Marketing from Indiana State University and a M.A. in Integrated Marketing Communications from St. Bonaventure University. Along with putting her marketing knowledge into everyday practice, Megan also shares her talents with up and coming professionals as an adjunct professor at St. Bonaventure University's IMC program. The joy of teaching inspired the creation of "The Marketist Academy," a premier coaching program designed to give companies, from marketing associates to owners and CEOs, the tools and knowledge they need to grow as business creators.

Just after beginning her marketing business as a "side job" in 2015, Megan's full-time career came to abrupt halt when she found herself out of a job as a communications director. The stress, anxiety and uncertainty that she felt in the days, weeks and months afterwards inspired her to write this book.

The southwestern Indiana native has a passion to create—from paintings and photography to writing and building her family tree through genealogical research, she finds inspiration in a variety of outlets outside of the marketing communications industry. She resides in Lancaster, NY with her husband Ben and dog, Sammy.

[LIKE MEGAN'S PAGE ON FACEBOOK](#)
[FOLLOW MEGAN ON TWITTER](#)
[FOLLOW MEGAN ON INSTAGRAM](#)
[VIEW MEGAN'S OTHER PROJECTS ONLINE](#)

Love the book? Please leave a review!

Thank you for downloading my book! I really appreciate all of your feedback, and we love hearing what you have to say. I need your input to make the next version better. Please leave a helpful REVIEW on Amazon by turning the page. Thanks so much!

—Megan

How I Did It

NOW IT'S YOUR TURN

Discover the EXACT 3-step blueprint you need to become
a bestselling author in 3 months.

Self-Publishing School helped me, and now I want them to help you with this FREE VIDEO SERIES!

Even if you're busy, bad at writing, or don't know where to start, you CAN write a bestseller and build your best life.

With tools and experience across a variety niches and professions, Self-Publishing School is the <u>only</u> resource you need to
take your book to the finish line!

DON'T WAIT

Watch this FREE VIDEO SERIES now, and
say "YES" to becoming a bestseller:

https://xe172.isrefer.com/go/curcust/mwagner930

Credits:

Cover Design: Rick Koston
Author Photos: Rich Borosky at Big Beat Creative Studios
Editing: Spencer Borup at Nerdy Wordsmith Ink

Made in the USA
Middletown, DE
09 September 2022